BLACK AND BRAVE HISTORY

30 SHEROES

WHO SHOOK BRITAIN

WRITTEN BY ANU ADEBOGUN
ILLUSTRATED BY JOSEPHINE OLUYITAN

Cover design by Rita Sri Harningsih
Interior design by Monica Paterson
Illustrations by Josephine Oluyitan

ISBN: 978-1-7398084-0-2 (Paperback)
ISBN: 978-1-7398084-1-9 (Hardcover)

Published by Brave Ink Global

The Bristol Office
2nd Floor 5 High Street
Westbury On Trym
Bristol
England
BS9 3BY

Mum,
my first shero.
For your love, light and prayers.
Your gentle yet unwavering spirit
offering strength to myself and countless women,
time and time again.

Dad,
for loudly celebrating your only girl-child,
believing in the power of women,
and teaching the values of an educated mind and
grounded spirit.
You remind me always that I am equal, capable,
loved and lovable.

I cherish you both.

TABLE OF CONTENT

BLACK SHEROES:
SAVING LIVES, SAVING BRITIAN

INTRODUCTION

Dear Reader,

You are about to begin a journey of discovery, inspiration and celebration through the lives of 30 sheroes who shook Britain. A shero is a woman admired for her courage and outstanding achievement. She is brave and relentless. She is not moved by how society defines perfection; she creates her own standard, and her only competition is who she was yesterday. A shero is not superhuman; she is wonderfully human. She has strengths, weaknesses and everything in between, but she radically embraces herself. Every day she decides to love and accept herself, to give herself space to get it wrong, to do better and become her best self. A shero plots, plans, hopes and works hard at her goals. When challenges arise and failure happens, she may cry at the frustration of it all, but she will persist because she knows her dreams are worth it.

This book is not just about reading the achievements of phenomenal women. You are the purpose of this book. It is here to serve your goals and dreams, to remind you that you are not alone in your desire to shake things up. Your growth, dreams and goals can share centre stage with the sheroes who have gone before. Some even trailblazed the path for your gifts to shine. In this book, you will meet 30 of the many brave Black women who have shaken up Britain. I hope you are inspired by their journeys, learn and grow from them, understand the challenges they faced and will be in awe of their brave legacies. I challenge you to be brave. I dare you to chase your dreams.

Warmly,
Anu

AUTHOR'S NOTE

This book celebrates Black female presence in Britain.

Growing up as a young Black girl in Hackney during the early 2000s, life on a council estate was bleak. By the age of ten, I could notice the syringes and needles littered in parks and playgrounds, the strong smell of weed that hoovered throughout our block of flats. As postcode wars increased, my outside playtime reduced. The streets were no longer safe for hopscotch, skipping or playing the cheeky knock down ginger game. Getting lost in a book was the way I found to escape the world around me. It was the force I used to shut out the fear that was so real in our neighbourhood.

Another force of positivity in my childhood was learning about Black women doing important things. Whether they were actors, journalists, writers or teachers, it was powerful seeing them excel in their element. And it was a reminder that I, too, could become something. I could dream of a life beyond Clapton Square. Eventually, I realised that many of the awesome Black women I watched growing up were either African American (That's So Raven anybody?) or actresses in a Nollywood movie. What about the Black women, past and present, trailblazing in Britain? Black history should not just be about the struggle endured by a people. It should also celebrate their achievement and impact despite the discrimination and disadvantages they faced. Black history is brave history. And it is not solely American or African — it is British too.

3

Poet

Phillis was kidnapped at seven years old from West Africa. She was enslaved and brought to a slave market in Boston. Wrapped around her small frame was the only piece of clothing she owned: a dirty, stained carpet. She was exposed, alone, without hope and unsure of her destiny. She was eventually bought by the Wheatleys for less than a penny. As a child slave, Phillis wasn't allowed to attend school, but she had a natural talent for writing. She would write on everything — walls, paper and even doors. Her pen was anything her hands could find, whether a piece of chalk or charcoal. Phillis did not have an audience to praise her work or a teacher to give it a top grade. She didn't write to be recognised. Her love for writing kept her hope alive. The Wheatleys noticed Phillis's commitment and flair in writing and gave her a basic education. She set reading and writing goals for herself to ensure she continued to progress. After only 18 months in school, Phillis had achieved mastery in reading and could read the whole Bible with ease. She developed an interest in learning Latin and quickly achieved her goal to master the challenging language. Phillis wrote her first poem when she was only 13 years old. It was the beginning of a writing career that would bring her international recognition.

By 18 years old, Phillis had written a collection of 28 poems that she wanted to publish. However, newspapers in Boston were unwilling to support the work of an unknown African girl. Determined not to give up on her dreams of becoming a published poet, Phillis set her sights on London in search of a publishing deal. She sent copies of her poems far and wide until they reached Selina Hastings, the Countess of Huntingdon. The Countess was moved by Phillis's soulful poems and invited her to England. Phillis arrived in 1773, and the Countess instructed booksellers to help publish her collection. Phillis was only 19 years old when she published her first book, a collection of 39 poems. She became the first Black woman to have her book published in London, and it was bestseller in British society. There were raving reviews in The London Magazine, Westminster Magazine, London Chronicle and the Gentleman's Magazine. Phillis was curious and consistent in her craft. Her passion and diligence took her from writing on walls to becoming a successful published poet. Slaveowners could not ignore the writing on the wall (quite literally). Phillis was able to advocate for her right to education and go on to achieve success. Her words formed her path to becoming widely known. She had been kidnapped, enslaved and sold for nothing, but despite all odds, Phillis rose to become more than society's wildest expectation of her. You are never too young, or old, to shake off your past and redesign your future.

REFLECTIVE SPACE

- Write down your dreams and find a place to display them.
- What are you curious about or curious to learn?
- How can being consistent help fulfil your dreams?

Fanny Eaton
1835 – 1924

5

Victorian model

Fanny was born in Jamaica and arrived in London with her mum in the 1840s, right at the beginning of Queen Victoria's reign. Fanny began her professional life working as a servant in St Pancras and then worked as a charwoman for many years. Over time, she soon had ten young mouths she needed to feed. Determined to find more ways to support her family, Fanny saw art modelling as an opportunity for additional income. In the Victorian era, beauty standards were defined by tiny waists, porcelain white features and long silky hair.

Different hues, shades and skin tones were not considered beautiful or reflected in popular art. With high cheekbones, warm melanated skin and bouncy curls, Fanny did not fit the Victorian standard of beauty. However this did not stop her from working as a model at the Royal Academy of Art. Fanny looked different from what was considered beautiful during the Victorian Era, but bravely she took the opportunity to model and in doing so, helped make Victorian art more inclusive.

Fanny's face first appeared in a delicate graphite drawing by Simeon Solomon in 1859, which was displayed in The Fitzwilliam Museum in the University of Cambridge. In 1860, Fanny was featured in a Royal Academy Exhibition called The Mother of Moses. These two works changed her life by bringing national attention to her beauty, which then opened more doors for modelling opportunities. Around that time, several popular painters and artists had come together to form a creative group called the Pre–Raphaelites. They were passionate about creating art that was bold, daring and celebrated differences. The Pre–Raphaelites thought art in the Victorian era was becoming mechanical and predictable. They wanted to create a new, radical way of making art, and Fanny became their source of inspiration. As her popularity grew, she was featured in several artworks over the years. Each painting captured Fanny as her authentic self – a young Black mum and maid. She became one of the most visible women of colour to be immortalized through paintings in the Victorian era. Today, you can find paintings of her in the British Museum in London, National Museum in Wales and in America, at the Delaware Art Museum and the Yale Centre for British Art.

REFLECTIVE SPACE

🌀 Do you ever feel it is difficult to show up as your true self? How can you dare to be seen?

🌀 Write down 20 things you love about yourself. Celebrate beauty as you define it!

Evelyn Dove
1902–1987

Cabaret Singer

From a young age, Evelyn knew exactly what she wanted from life — and that was to create music to perform in major jazz and cabaret shows all over the world. She got into the Royal Academy of Music at only 15 years old and graduated after two years with a silver medal. She was diligent in her work and never failed to practice training her voice. She even built strength in her legs so she could dance for hours without getting tired. Unfortunately, she faced criticism at home. Her father, Francis, was a well-known barrister and wanted her to continue his legacy, but Evelyn would not give up her dreams. In response, he disowned her, leaving Evelyn even more isolated in a world that saw her as different. Despite being very talented and having trained at the best school, several London-based concert organisers shut their doors to her music because she was different from the performers they'd had before. So she created her own stage and took up a lead role in cabaret and jazz. She persisted and made music that allowed her to be true to herself — expressive, daring and bold.

Evelyn surrounded herself with people who helped her grow and wanted to see her dreams flourish. She found a community when she joined the Southern Syncopated Orchestra, a group of talented British West Indian, West African and Black American musicians.

They were a successful group and received invitations to perform at Buckingham Palace. In 1920, the orchestra travelled by ship to perform in a show, but the vessel had a ghastly crash. 35 members lost their lives at sea. Evelyn was fortunate to escape with her life. This near-death incident inspired her to live boldly in honour of her friends who had passed away. By 1925, she was a household name across Britain and a headline cabaret performer. A woman with a vision, Evelyn was strategic and teamed up with several bands, including The Chocolate Kiddies and Her Plantation Creoles, to build her brand presence. Every performance was met with roaring applause and a standing ovation. Not only did Evelyn share her talent with the world, she used it to trailblaze new paths in Britain. She was the first Black singer to perform her music on BBC Radio, which opened doors for other Black women to enter the industry.

She partnered with Edric Connor in a variety show to promote Black artists in Britain and starred in dramas and West End musicals. Evelyn stayed true to herself and pursued her dreams even when her family denied their support. For every rejection she received, Evelyn gave herself even more space to grow. Eventually, she found her place in jazz, cabaret and musical theatre and a community that would cheer her on to glory.

REFLECTIVE SPACE

- Being told 'no' can be a crushing blow. How can you bounce back after experiencing rejection?
- Do you have people in your life that uplift you when things get hard? Write down their names.
- How can you let them know you appreciate the support they offer?

Pauline Henriques
1914—1998

Actress, Justice of the Peace

As a child, Pauline would get excited when her family gathered in the living room to read plays together. She was a natural performer and took every chance to practice. It was an unforgettable display of energy whenever she performed. At 18, with her parents' encouragement, she enrolled at the London Academy of Music and Dramatic Art. She auditioned for several productions and was determined to perfect her craft. However, the only roles they offered her were of maids and mammies. Pauline believed she could take centre stage with a lead role, but she was ignored. To play Lady Macbeth in one production, Pauline was instructed to wear a 'white face'. This meant she had to put on theatrical makeup to make herself look like a white person. The industry placed immense pressure on Black women to 'white up' in order to get lead roles. Between the frustration with the unfairness of it all and feeling tired of only being offered one-line roles as a Black maid, Pauline left college discouraged. But she kept acting. She saw every role as an opportunity to improve herself. Even for the one-line roles, she gave it her all. Her hard work paid off, and her big break came in 1946 when she landed a lead role as Hattie Harris in the play *All God's Chillun Got Wings* by Eugene O'Neil.

For the first time in British history, a Black woman confidently graced the screen. Pauline became the first Black actress on British TV, where theatre was only just being streamed into British homes. Pauline continued to soar in her career and performed everywhere, from leading theatres to welfare halls.

In 1956, Pauline was called to feature in the groundbreaking BBC drama documentary titled *A Man from the Sun*. It was the first in TV history to explore the lives of the Caribbean women and men who had accepted the government's invitation to settle in Britain and rebuild the nation. Pauline later trained as a counsellor, campaigner and advocate for young women who had experienced abuse and homelessness. She had a big heart for her community and was passionate about creating opportunities for marginalised groups in Britain. The Queen of England recognised her service with distinguished honorary awards. Pauline was a pioneer and pacesetter both in the world of performance and social justice. She knew she had more to offer than playing 'the black maid'. So she kept practicing her craft and pushing for opportunities until she became the first Black woman to perform on British TV. Outside of performance, Pauline used her voice to speak for young women who were isolated, defenceless and judged by society. She later became the first Black female Justice of the Peace and magistrate in the UK.

REFLECTIVE SPACE

◎ How will you use your voice to promote your potential?

◎ How can your voice advocate for others?

11

Wordsmith, Publisher

Margaret had a multicultural upbringing: her mother was from the Fanti tribe in Ghana, Africa, and her father was born in Barbados in the Caribbean. Little Margaret grew up fascinated by the world and obsessed with words and books. As a teen, she met Clive Allison, a budding poet. Since they were both working together, they decided to launch their own publishing company, Allison & Busby Ltd. At only 20 years old, Margaret became the youngest woman and first Black person to establish a publishing company in Britain. Running this business was a big responsibility that required a huge amount of work.

The company did not have a lot of money, and Margaret knew her first customers wouldn't either, but like her, they were dreamers with pockets full of hope and minds eager to learn. So Margaret published poetry in affordable paperback books. News of Margaret's publishing company spread across Britain and beyond. Sam Greenlee was an aspiring African American author who had been rejected by 40 publishers in the US and the UK. When he heard of Margaret's company, he travelled to Britain to meet her and share his manuscript, *The Spook Who Sat by The Door*. Margaret believed in Sam's book and took a chance that no other publisher would. She made this book her company's first full-length novel. It became a bestseller in Britain within a year and later went on to become an international bestseller and even a movie.

With her success as a publisher, Margaret was inspired to revisit her first passion: writing. She reflected on her identity of being British, Ghanaian and Caribbean and how she had never studied any novels, poems or stories written by Black women while at university. She wanted to find a way to celebrate the diverse experiences of Black women across continents, drawing attention to how they are uniquely special and cannot all fit into one box. In 1992, she asked over 200 Black women from around the world to put their thoughts, feelings and experiences into words. Phenomenal writers like Maya Angelou, Toni Morrison and Alice Walker responded to Margaret's call. Collecting their voices together, Margaret published a pioneering book called *The Daughters of Africa*. It was the first anthology of its kind in the world. Almost three decades later, Margaret updated the anthology, creating the *New Daughters of Africa* to celebrate a new generation of young Black female writers.

The new edition was published in 2019 with a powerful mission to give a young woman living in Africa a full scholarship to study in Britain. For a long time, the traditional publishing industry in Britain was known to be exclusive, with little representation of Black people and other ethnic groups in their work. The success of Margaret's book showcasing Black female experiences and her success in publishing Sam Greenlee's book opened up a path for more Black people to have their thoughts published, printed and enjoyed by readers across the world.

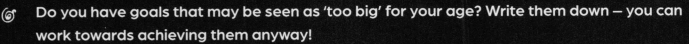

REFLECTIVE SPACE

- Do you have goals that may be seen as 'too big' for your age? Write them down — you can work towards achieving them anyway!
- Search online and find five young women in the world right now doing incredible things.

Opera Singer, Composer

Amanda was fascinated with voice, music and composing. She was raised in an atmosphere of creativity and music. Her father, Ira Aldridge, was a popular Black actor, and her mother Amanda Pauline, was a Swedish opera singer. Amanda's father died when she was only 17 months old, but he left behind an inspiring legacy as the first Black man to play the lead roles of Macbeth and King Lear in Shakespeare's plays. Although Amanda's passion was music and not theatre performance, her father's achievements inspired her to define greatness for herself. Her first major gig came when she was only 15 years old, when she sang at an orchestra in Crystal Palace. At 17, Amanda entered a singing competition and won a scholarship to study at the Royal College of Music. She started college in 1883 and was a pupil of Jenny Lind, a talented opera singer of that time. Under Jenny's instruction, Amanda developed her contralto voice. She sang and sang, filling up every inch of space with her powerful voice. Typically, you heard Amanda before you saw her.

But one day, her voice box became inflamed with laryngitis.

Amanda desperately tried to sing again, but her voice was gone — and she never would recover. Her career as an opera singer may have been over, but her love for music was not. Amanda said, 'Life without music would be unbearable, I cannot keep still. So many things are happening that I must be active to see it all.' She published her compositions under the pen name Montague Ring to separate her composing work from the various other roles she juggled. The public adored her songs, and they were promoted by major publishing firms across London. Her instrumentals were played by orchestras and military bands everywhere. Her most famous compositions were 'Three African Dances' (1913), 'Three Arabian Dances' (1919) and 'Carnival Suit of Five Dances' (1924). Today, most of her work can be found at the British Public Library in London. Amanda became an excellent music teacher, and her students went on to shock the world with their exceptional musical talent. Three of her Black students, Marian Anderson, Roland Hayes and Paul Robeson, were known as powerful freedom singers and acclaimed artists in the 20th century. Amanda was a curator of sounds and melodies. Her love of music was deep, her talent undeniable and her work ethic, even at 87, unmatched. Amanda found and created new ways to continue speaking the language she loved most — music.

REFLECTIVE SPACE

It is important to not allow curveballs or failures to hold us back from doing what we love. What are some setbacks you have faced in pursuing your goals? How can you overcome them? What can you try to do differently?

List out some of your passions. What are the different ways to do these things you love? For example, if you love playing a sport or dancing, would you ever consider coaching or training others to play as well? If you enjoy public speaking, would you ever consider starting a podcast or being an MC at events?

Global Entertainer

Cassandra loved the world of creativity, comedy, music and dance and began performing at the age of three. She travelled across England with her father to act and sing in Uncle Tom's Cabin shows. In media and entertainment, Black women were often presented as 'exotic' beings. As Cassandra built her career, people struggled to acknowledge her talent without first commenting on how her being 'coloured' somehow took away from it. Cassandra rose above the backhanded compliments. By 1907, Cassie was famous for wearing the most classy, elaborate costumes at her performances. Once, she went through 50 stages outfits in just one show!

By 1928, Cassie was opening up and headlining shows at the New Opera House in Christchurch, New Zealand. Every one of her shows ended with an encore, especially when she sang her famous song 'Moving Day'. During the First World War, Cassie's music played on the radio and filtered into British homes, filling them with laughter and melody. Cassandra was a force of sophistication, comedy and class. Music was her transport from Brixton to the world stage, where she brought music, dance and comedy into the lives of many. Through her fabulous and colourful costumes, she was unapologetically herself as she showcased Black culture to the world. With Cassandra's legacy, it is no surprise that to this day, London hotspots like Brixton and Camden are where music, culture and diversity mix and are celebrated.

REFLECTIVE SPACE

⊙ List at least three different ways you can showcase yourself and your culture. It could be how you choose to style your hair, the unique clothes you wear or even proudly introducing others to your language.

⊙ The world is your global stage. If you could travel anywhere in the world to do what you enjoy, which country would it be? Add at least two to your travel bucket list.

Kanya King
1969

17

Businesswoman, Founder

Born in north London, Kanya's whole childhood revolved around her block of flats in Kilburn. Her father died when she was 13, leaving her mother alone to raise her and her eight siblings. Kanya started working to support her mum with extra money. At 16 years old, Kanya dropped out of school after becoming pregnant. She was a teen mom, but Kanya believed that her best years were ahead. She went back to school and completed her degree in English Literature at Goldsmith University. After graduating, she worked as a TV and media researcher and organised small-scale R&B and reggae concerts in London. Kanya loved listening to music, and it bothered her how negatively Black people were presented in the media and that the music she danced to at home was never played on the radio or TV. Black music was both a beautiful art form and tool of empowerment that Kanya envisioned showcasing to British society and the world.

She came up with an idea for a media platform called the Music of Black Origin (MOBO) Awards. Kanya shared her idea with several people but received discouraging feedback that Black music wouldn't sell, or that the media would never get behind it. Kanya remained committed to building this platform. She did not have a lot of money and against everyone's advice, remortgaged her house to fund the first MOBO Awards because she believed in her vision.

One day while working a shift at Arsenal Football Club, Kanya helped a flustered man find his young nephew. While they waited, Kanya shared her big dreams for the MOBO Awards. Little did she know she was speaking to one of the directors of ITV Network. She secured a broadcast slot to have the MOBO Awards on TV! However, she only had six weeks to put the event together and had never organised anything this big before. But Kanya, as always, was determined to give it her best.

The MOBO Awards launched officially in 1996. It was the first Black awards show in Europe and was broadcasted to 250 million people. Kanya had worried no one would show up on the day, but people came in droves! Important guests like former Prime Minister Tony Blair and international superstar Lionel Richie were present. For over 20 years, the MOBO awards shone a spotlight on fresh Black British talent like Ms. Dynamite, Estelle, Craig David, Krept and Konan, Stormzy and many more. Since then, the platform, has expanded to support a trust that gives opportunities to talented young people, promote health awareness campaigns, encourage blood donations, and connect Black British talent to careers and mentors in the creative industry through their new platform Mobolise. Kanya, at one time, was a teen mom and school dropout, but she remained determined to lead an impactful and successful life. When society failed to recognise Black talent, Kanya risked it all to give Black British music a stage.

REFLECTIVE SPACE

ⓒ According to Kanya, success did not come easy — but she refused to quit and saw every obstacle as an opportunity. Think of a difficult time or rejection that motivated you to strive harder. What did that experience teach you?

ⓒ What are ways you can begin to see obstacles as opportunities?

18

Olympic Gold Athlete

When Tessa was six, her family moved from Jamaica to the UK. There was a lot of racial tension in the UK during that time and her parents warned her that people would call her mean names, but still she was shocked by the level of hate and racism she experienced. Fortunately, Tessa had a strong community around her. Tessa was 14 when she first handled a javelin. Her friends made a bet over a bag of crisps on who could throw it farthest and Tessa won! She joined the local sports team, quickly rising through the ranks, and signed up for the Wolverhampton & Bliston Athletics Club to compete in javelin and other disciplines. At 16, Tessa won a sports award for javelin at the English Schools' Athletics Championships — the first of many awards and distinctions in her athletic career. At the European Athletics Championships, Tessa broke the UK javelin throw junior record five times. In 1976, she became the national record holder and the youngest Olympic javelin competitor at 20 years old. Two years later, she won her first major gold medal in the Commonwealth Games. The wins continued, but tragically, Tessa suffered a major injury — a ruptured Achilles tendon and a broken bone in her throwing arm. After nearly two years of recuperating from surgery, Tessa thought she had healed enough for the World Championships, but sadly she reinjured her Achilles tendon. She was back in action a year later for the 1984 Summer Olympics, where she made history winning the Gold Medal in the javelin throw.

It was Britain's first Olympic win in the sport since the beginning of the modern Olympics in the 19th century!

Following her victory and win for Britain, Tessa received racist letters saying she could never truly be British because she was Black. She also lost her job, leaving her with no income or sponsorship. While doing promotional work at sports events, Tessa learned she was being paid only £1,000 to speak at these events — while white women athletes were being paid ten times that amount. This unfair pay gap made her furious and she decided to boycott further events until a new deal could be struck. She spoke up about this injustice and continues to challenge the discrimination and sexism that prevents women athletes from being paid the same as men.

In over 20 years of competition, Tessa had done the unthinkable! She was the first and only British woman to compete at six successive Olympic Games. She was the British Athletics Writers' Association Athlete of the Year in 1977, 1978 and 1984. She also served as the Vice-Chairman of Sport England, started an academy in Newham to train athletes to represent Britain in the 2012 Summer Olympic and Paralympic Games, was placed in the England Athletics Hall of Fame, and received several honours from the Queen of England for her Olympic Gold Medal, her charity work and her services to Sport England. Tessa broke barriers and paved the way for other Black female athletes — both on and off the track.

REFLECTIVE SPACE

⚲ Write out one thing that really stands out to you from Tessa's experiences. What do these experiences say about Tessa's character?

⚲ What can you learn from Tessa's response to challenges she faced?

Paralympic Wheelchair Racer, Activist

Anne was born in Mihuu, Kenya and was struck with polio at the age of 2, leaving her paralysed from her waist down. The village treated her as an outcast due to poor understanding of polio as an illness — they thought Anne had been cursed, that she'd spread the disease to the rest of the village, and they called her a snake, because her disability meant she had to crawl on the ground using her upper body to move around. As Anne grew up, the most important thing to her was getting an education. Schools in Kenya at that time were not accessible and Anne was not able to participate in P.E; she had to sit on the sidelines while everyone else was active and running around. She attended university with the goal of becoming a teacher. In April 2000, she came to Britain to get her master's in educational psychology so that she could support young people with special needs. But when Anne had her first son, she found life in a new country as a new mum with a disability a little too much to bear and began going to the gym for self-care and her wellbeing. There, she was introduced to the exciting phenomenon of wheelchair racing. In 2004, Anne became the first person from Kenya and Sub-Saharan Africa to compete in wheelchair racing at the Paralympics in Athens.

Over the next three years, Anne created a new identity for herself as a power competitor in wheelchair racing, travelling all around the world to compete. When the Olympic Games came to London in 2012, she took part in the torch relay.

Now, Anne competes in the T54 racing category as a British athlete and campaigns for the rights of disabled individuals. She sits as a board member for UK Athletics, British Paralympics Association, Active Essex and Sports Chaplaincy UK; she is the only Black person to be involved across all major sport boards. She advocates for diversity and inclusion efforts to include women with disabilities. Anne also founded the Olympia-Wafula Foundation, where she promotes healthy living solutions to enrich the lives of people with disabilities. In Kenya, Anne works to provide wheelchairs and scholarships to young people with disabilities who, like Anne once did, want to go to school. Anne's journey is one of courage and strength.

She was once a little girl with a disease that made it impossible for her to walk and she became a strong Paralympic athlete. Her wheelchair became a source of empowerment, helping Anne in her race for a better life. Now, Anne continues to use her courage and determination to challenge the misconceptions and stigma around disability.

REFLECTIVE SPACE

What do you find most inspiring about Anne's story?

Disability can be an important and positive part of a person's identity. How can you show love, respect and appreciation to people who have different abilities to your own?

Protégée to the Lord Chief Justice

Dido was born mixed race; her father, John Lindsay, was a Royal Navy Captain and her mother, Maria, was an African slave. Dido often felt like she was living on the outside looking in, uninvited and never quite belonging. Left motherless at the age of three, her father took her to England to live with his uncle, the 8th Earl of Mansfield and the Lord Chief Justice. He was a strong orator and highly respected judge who showed Dido much kindness. When Thomas Hutchinson, the Governor of Massachusetts, came to Kenwood House, he noticed how the judge showed much affection to Dido and frequently requested her assistance. Dido was inquisitive, smart and showed great leadership potential. She was put in charge of key matters around the estate and soon became a protégée to the Lord Chief Justice.

Dido's presence at Kenwood House and closeness to Lord Mansfield may have had a powerful impact on two of his landmark cases against slavery.

In the Somerset case, Lord Mansfield ruled for the freedom of an African slave called Somerset, who had been badly beaten and was to be deported to Jamaica. Slavery abolitionists used Lord Mansfield's ruling in the Somerset case to campaign for the freedom of enslaved people in Britain. The second case was the tragedy of the Zong slave ship, where 132 children, men and women had been thrown overboard so that the insurers could receive compensation for lost cargo. The case was brought to Lord Mansfield, who declared that no human being could be insured, not even if they were poor or enslaved. His judgment challenged the existence of the slave trade.

Dido's life was made into an award-winning film called *Belle* by British-Ghanaian filmmaker Amma Asante MBE. A beautiful painting of Dido and Elizabeth Murray hangs on the elegant walls of Scone Palace. Dido was a bright influential girl of mixed background in a world unprepared for her. Even though she grew up not knowing where she belonged, she found a way to leave a lasting legacy.

REFLECTIVE SPACE

Placing home was difficult for Dido Belle and belonging felt unachievable. Dido teaches us that home is wherever our hearts will it to be, and with whoever chooses to honour us, no matter how different we may seem. It can be scary to feel like the odd one out in a particular space. What can you do to feel powerful and confident in those situations?

Sometimes it can be hard to talk to the people we're close to about important issues. How can you find the courage to speak up for what is right?

Abolitionist, Writer

Mary Prince was born in Bermuda in a time where Black children were sold into slavery for as little as eight pounds. Mary stood alongside her family in a marketplace and was sold into the cold, calloused hands of slave masters. She was only ten when she saw her family for the last time. For 17 hours every day, Mary would work in salt ponds under the burning sun. She had the impossible task of collecting salt crystals from the murky water, which gave her blisters, boils and sores that grew worse as the years went on. Hard beatings and cutting words seemed to be the only certainty and companion in the beginning of Mary's lonely life. Mary was sold four times before arriving in Britain. She managed to escape to join the anti-slavery society in London.

Mary had been a freewoman for only one year when in 1829, she took a brave step to write a petition to Parliament to abolish slavery within all British colonies.

She became the first woman to present an anti-slavery petition to Parliament. Mary's first petition was rejected by Parliament, but this did not deter her. She strengthened her alliances by working with other abolitionists across Britain, sharing her harrowing experience of slavery. Mary wanted to go back to Bermuda to find her family, but because slavery was still legal, there was a risk she could be captured and re-enslaved if she returned.

In 1831, Mary wrote her autobiography *The History of Mary Prince: A West Indian Slave*. She became the first Black woman to ever publish an autobiography in Britain, and her memoir published three editions in the first year alone. Mary held nothing back when writing her story. It moved the hearts of Britons everywhere and became a potent tool for the anti-slavery movement. When Mary's story of struggle, suffering and slavery finally broke free, it helped liberate others. A child-slave turned freedom writer; Mary showed that the power of a woman's pen can be greater than the sword.

REFLECTIVE SPACE

Write about a difficult experience or challenge you have had to overcome. How has this impacted you?

Once you get comfortable with writing down your story, you can develop the courage to share it. Sharing your story is a powerful way to connect to others and bring about real change. Who might you share your story with?

27

Activist, Journalist

Claudia was eight years old when her family migrated from Trinidad to America to escape poverty. Her parents thought America would bring them good fortune, but soon they found themselves facing the oppression of Jim Crow laws and segregation. Their unsafe living worsened Claudia's tuberculosis, causing irreparable damage to her lungs from which she never recovered. Despite her ill health, Claudia left school and worked in a laundry, millinery and factory to support her family. Her interests in politics and social justice began around this time. She started writing for the Negro Nationalist newspaper and shared her political views under her own column called 'Claudia's Comments'. For the next decade, Claudia dedicated her life to a youth movement in Harlem that campaigned against the struggles of the American working class. She believed working-class people could lead and that women should be empowered. As a political activist, she pushed for equal pay, job training programmes and wartime childcare programmes.

Her work as an activist was very dangerous. Many powerful people disagreed with her political views. In order to ensure her safety, she had to change her name from Claudia Vera Cumberbatch and operated as Claudia Jones. Even with these measures, she was arrested and imprisoned four times throughout her life. Because of her tuberculosis, Claudia had her first heart attack in prison. In 1950, the American government threatened Claudia with deportation.

Her birth country, Trinidad, refused to allow her to return because they thought Claudia was too troublesome. Claudia left America and was allowed entry into the UK for humanitarian reasons. She continued to campaign against racism in education, employment and housing. She also campaigned for the release of Nelson Mandela and against the Commonwealth Immigrant Bill, which made it difficult for non-white people to migrate to Britain. In 1958, Claudia founded Britain's first Black newspaper, the West Indian Gazette. The newspaper raised awareness of the Black experience and encouraged peace between people of the Commonwealth and world at large.

The year 1958 was also a time of great strife in London, when crowds of white youth armed themselves to terrorise Black people and destroy their homes in the Notting Hill race riots. The riots lasted a week and 140 people, mainly white, were arrested. In response to these devastating events, Claudia suggested the Black community have a carnival to celebrate their heritage. She secured St Pancras Town Hall, and the carnival was nationally televised. The money made from the carnival was used to cover the fines of the young people involved in the riots. This was the beginning of what is now known as the Notting Hill Carnival, the largest annual Caribbean celebration in London. Claudia lived a life of impact on both sides of the Atlantic, in America and Britain. She used her voice to champion the causes of her community and amplify the voice of her people. Her health was a continuous concern throughout her life, but still she left a powerful legacy through her exceptional political activism, campaigns and community organizing.

REFLECTIVE SPACE

Even as we chase our dreams and work towards becoming people of impact, our health and wellness is very important. What are the ways you can practice self-care and take better care of your health today?

What are some causes you care about? How can you speak up about them?

Gloria Cumper
1922–1995

29

Lawmaker, First Black Woman at Cambridge

Gloria's father, W.A Carpenter, was a land surveyor who built Jamaica's first canal. He believed in the potential of his daughters and invested in their education by sending them to school in England. At 13, Gloria arrived in Britain and attended a grammar school for girls called the Mary Datchelor School. Gloria thrived at school – she was always raising her hand, asking questions, and eager to share her thoughts with anyone who would listen. She decided she would become a barrister and use her confidence, sharp thinking and impressive speech to push for justice in every case. She studied law in Canada at the University of Toronto during World War II. As the first Caribbean student there, it was an isolating experience. When the war ended, Gloria sailed back to England to continue her legal studies at the University of Cambridge, where she was the first Black woman ever admitted! This was an incredible opportunity, but also a daunting experience.

Gloria was visibly different and as a black woman, she was a minority in that space. When Gloria met George Cumper at university, the pair fell in love and married, but not everyone was pleased. One of her tutors warned that by marrying George, who was white, Gloria would hinder his progress as an aspiring economist. His white family also refused to accept Gloria.

Microaggressions and rejections plagued much of her early adulthood, but she continued to trust her abilities and work hard. Gloria graduated with a first class degree in law and was called to the Bar at Middle Temple Inn in 1947. Excitedly, Gloria moved back to Jamaica with her family to begin her legal practice, but was disappointed when no one wanted to hire a woman to join their private practice. Instead, she became a tutor of law and established the law faculty at the University of the West Indies. Her mission remained the same: to advocate for the rights of the vulnerable and bring about social change through law.

Gloria challenged old laws that risked the human rights of children. She transformed legislation previously allowing men to neglect the welfare of their 'illegitimate' children. Gloria set up the family court in Jamaica to ensure families could easily access justice and get support for their children. Gloria's reforms helped to secure the rights of children and families in Jamaica and across the Commonwealth. Gloria was a Black woman who achieved many firsts. As the first Black woman to attend Cambridge University, she was very visible and this came with unwanted attention. But Gloria did not make herself small or hide away while there. She was bold, actively involved in student community and finished her studies with excellence. Gloria then went on to use her knowledge of the law to make social change across the Commonwealth. She shows that while being the first to do anything may be daunting, it can trailblaze a path for others.

REFLECTIVE SPACE

What will you be the first to do in your family? It could be going to university, working a professional job or even starting your own business. Whatever it may be, write it down and put it where you will always be reminded.

Write down an affirmation of your purpose. Here are some examples: 'Even if no one has done it before, I can challenge myself to be the first' or 'I can do hard things, I will be proof that it is possible'.

Community Activist

Olive was born in St Catherine, Jamaica and moved to south London at the age of nine. After a negative experience at school, she left without any certificates, though she later returned to college while balancing a full-time job. One dry and cool November evening when Olive was 17, she was walking down Brixton High Street when she caught sight of a policeman arresting a Nigerian diplomat for driving a nice car. The officer had suspected the diplomat had stolen the Mercedes, because he could not believe a Black man could afford one, and arrested and beat the man in front of his wife and children. Olive approached the scene, outraged by the racist and unjust arrest she had witnessed. But for trying to help, she was assaulted by the officers and later arrested. At the police station, she was forced to strip and was beaten. This horrendous incident stirred her to passionately fight for equality and human rights.

During the 1970s, Olive became a powerful force and joined a Black youth movement of West Africans and West Indians who fought against racism in Britain. They called themselves the British Black Panthers and their campaigns catered to the specific needs of Black people in the UK. Olive fought for squatter's rights in London and Manchester, while also setting up the Brixton Black Women's Group. She continued her education, studying social sciences at Manchester University, and started several projects to serve Black women, including the Manchester Black Women's Cooperative and Manchester Black Women's Mutual Aid Group. Sadly she died of blood cancer at the young age of 27. Although her life was cut short by illness, Olive lived fully and spent each day with purpose and in service to others. She also left a strong legacy: The Olive Morris Awards were established in 2008 to recognise young women of African descent ages 16 to 27 who are fighting for justice. Olive wanted to make the world a better place for working class people and as history reveals, she did just that.

REFLECTIVE SPACE

Olive had a short but remarkable life. Her superpower was her bravery. Life is too short to be wasted on second guessing yourself. List some of the ways you can be brave in your world.

There are many different ways to respond when you witness something unjust. What are some things you can do?

Justice Campaigner, Life Peer in the House of Lords

On 22 April 1993, Doreen received horrible news that her 18-year-old son Stephen had been murdered by a gang of racist young white boys in southeast London while he waited to catch his bus. The day after the murder, an anonymous letter was found in a telephone box naming the boys involved in the stabbing. It gave the police a strong lead, and Doreen hoped they would arrest the five boys involved and bring them to justice. However, the investigation stalled. In June 1993, the police searched the homes of the five suspects but only charged two, Neil Acourt and Luke Knight, who denied the charges. The following month, all charges were dropped. In December, Doreen's barrister presented new evidence for consideration, but the prosecution still refused to bring forward any new charges, claiming the new evidence was insufficient.

At this stage, Doreen and her family decided to put forward a private prosecution against Stephen's suspected killers at the Old Bailey. They had strong evidence, such as a video of the suspects using racist and violent language, but still Doreen's case for Stephen was considered insufficient. Doreen refused to give up and started a five-year-long nationwide campaign for justice.

This led to a public inquiry in 1998 to investigate how the police had dealt with racially motivated crime. The following year, Sir William MacPherson, a high court judge in England and Wales, published a 350-page report, which found evidence that the Metropolitan Police was institutionally racist and exposed that their investigation of Stephen's murder had been blotched, messy and insensitive.

Doreen and her family endured unthinkable pain, loss and several attempts to discredit their campaign for justice. After 19 years, two of the five suspects were found guilty of Stephen's murder. Doreen had waited for almost two decades to get this small amount of justice for her son. She set up the Stephen Lawrence Charitable Trust to help young people overcome barriers and disadvantages in school and society. Doreen was honoured by the Queen with an OBE for her services to community relations, her campaign against institutional racism and her work with young people. Doreen fought not only for Stephen but to give a voice to those who had lost their loved ones to the evils of racism. She became one of the most influential Black women in the UK and helped reform the justice system by speaking loudly about injustice. Doreen never stopped raising her voice and eventually British society was forced to listen.

REFLECTIVE SPACE

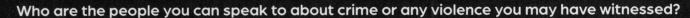

◎ Who are the people you can speak to about crime or any violence you may have witnessed?
◎ What injustice do you see in society that you can speak out about today?

UK's First Black High Court Judge

From early childhood, Linda stood out. She was bullied for being the only Black person in school, a horrible experience that made her resolve to see every human being treated with dignity and respect. As a teenager, Linda was fascinated with people like Nelson Mandela, who had risked it all for equality, and also unknown superheroes like one of her schoolteachers, who had fought against the apartheid in South Africa. They were 'doers', and that was exactly what Linda aspired to become. Linda went to law school and was called to the prestigious Bar of England and Wales in 1981. She successfully started building her legal practice by taking on criminal cases. Though she had earned her place at the bar, Linda often received rude and belittling comments — that the Attorney General was just taking on a 'token black' and that Linda was a 'coconut' (Black on the outside, white on the inside).

Linda faced a lot of challenges early in her career. One of her cases involved a man charged for drunk driving. Her client took one look at her, scowled and said: 'I told the solicitor I did not want a woman representing me.' Linda remained professional and won the case for her client, but after the hearing, he stormed off without a word of thanks. Other times, clerks would tell solicitors that Linda was unavailable for work so that the case would be given to a male pupil.

One clerk even advised her to 'white up' so potential clients couldn't 'tell the difference'. During this time, there were no formal ways of reporting discrimination, but Linda realised that despite these difficulties, she could contribute to real change and open the door for others in her profession. With diligence and determination, she proved her abilities and built an excellent reputation. In 2004, the Lord Chancellor asked her to be one of Her Majesty's Judges. Linda struggled with the decision — becoming a judge would mean starting all over again, albeit on a higher level, and she didn't know if the other judges would accept her. Eventually, she agreed.

For Linda's first sitting as a judge, the court was jam-packed with people watching her, curious to see how she would perform. The pressure was immense, but she found ways to carry herself through. Linda became the first Black high court judge in Britain and went on to serve in the judiciary for almost a decade, a landmark achievement. After Linda, it was seven years before another person of colour was made a high court judge. The Bar still has a long way to go to become as diverse and reflective of the society it serves. For her many contributions, Linda received the Eleanor Roosevelt Award and was featured on the *Powerlist* of influential Black Britons. She continues to support young people aspiring toward the Bar and inspires us to be confident in standing out in places that are not yet as diverse as they should be.

REFLECTIVE SPACE

◎ What keeps you in your comfort zone?
◎ Linda had to let go of her doubts and truly believe in her potential to become a judge.
What might you have to leave behind in order to move closer towards your goals?
List why you think it might be worth it in the end.

Politician, Diplomat, Educational Leader

Valerie immigrated to Britain with her family when she was nine years old. As a Black family living in Kent in the 1960s, they faced much racism from their neighbours. Valerie attended a girl's school in Bexleyheath and searched out positive ways to belong there. She joined the school choir because she loved music, but whenever they performed, Valerie would get many curious stares. After, people would gather around her, touching her hair and skin and making her feel different and uncomfortable. As she grew up, she focused on her studies and took on many responsibilities, even becoming the first Black deputy head girl at her school. She became interested in the issues affecting her community. She was passionate about challenging injustice in society and bringing about equality. She wanted to understand how social attitudes and cultures were formed. She went on to study sociology and cultural studies and completed her PhD at the University of East Anglia, for which she researched the challenging realities Black girls faced between leaving school and entering the work force.

From there, Valerie began her career in politics. She worked for the local government across several London boroughs, led in public sector roles as the Chief Executive of the Equal Opportunities Commission and became a member of Parliament. She was the first Black woman to become a cabinet minister and one of the first three Black people to ever ascend to the House of Lords.

She later became the Secretary of State for International Development. Valerie's determination to make equality a reality gave her opportunities to make an impact on a global scale too. She joined the United Nations as the Under-Secretary-General for Humanitarian Affairs and Emergency Relief, where she led missions to countries devastated by war and natural disasters. She then led a task force with the World Health Organisation to ensure humanitarian access in health emergencies. Valerie also became a patron of the Amos Bursary, an organisation founded in 2009 to help British African and Caribbean youth attend top universities, secure professional jobs and give back to society.

In 2015, Valerie achieved another milestone by becoming the first Black woman to ever lead a university in the UK as the director of SOAS. Within higher education institutions in the UK, Black women are underrepresented in leadership; among more than 100 different universities in the UK, there were only 25 Black female professors in 2018. As director of SOAS, Valerie went on to make monumental changes, working with the National Union of Students to challenge the inequality between white, Black and Asian students in their degree results. In 2020, she became the first Black person to lead a college at the University of Oxford as the Master of University College. Across professions and around the world, Valerie made an impressive impact and continues to inspire us today.

REFLECTIVE SPACE

- Like young Valerie, when you feel excluded or uninvited, in what ways can you remind yourself that it is okay to be unique?
- Valerie has attained many firsts in her long record of achievements, but it started with being the first Black head girl at her school. You might have a long list of goals you want to be the first to achieve. Highlight some of your goals that can be achieved sooner than later and set yourself some deadlines.

Patricia Scotland
1955

39

Patricia was encouraged by her father to have big aspirations like her brothers. She was a confident girl and was never afraid to ask grownups 'why?'. She challenged them to prove the fairness of any given situation, and so, her keen interest in social justice grew. At school, Patricia voiced her intentions to become a lawyer who fought for equality. Her announcement was met with great discouragement from her teachers. As a Black girl, Patricia did not fit the profile of those accepted into the Bar, so she was told to lower her ambitions. But Patricia dismissed their doubts and rose to the challenge of pursuing her goals.

Patricia went on to study law and successfully secured a pupillage. She handled a range of cases, from company law and public enquiries to family law cases in child abuse, international child abduction and domestic violence. Patricia was a fierce and robust advocate who refused to back down from an argument, and it did not go without notice. She became the youngest woman and first Black woman to become a Queen's Counsel barrister at the age of 35. She advocated for political change in a variety of issues and created a pro bono lawyers unit to ensure that British nationals imprisoned in foreign countries could get the legal support they required for free. Patricia refused to accept that money, or the lack of it, should be the reason anyone was denied justice.

In 1999, Patricia was appointed the Under-Secretary of State for the Foreign and Commonwealth Office, where she was responsible for keeping positive diplomatic relations between the British government and the Caribbean, North America and other overseas territories. She worked to reform the Commonwealth Office so that Britain could respond effectively to disasters and emergencies happening overseas. Patricia also created a forced marriage and international child abduction unit that has helped return thousands of abducted people back to the UK. In 2003, she became Minister of State for the Criminal Justice System. Under her leadership, domestic violence in Britain decreased by 64%, saving countless lives.

In 2007, Patricia was the first woman since the position was created in 1315 to become Attorney General in England and Wales. She established a partnership between England, Canada, America, New Zealand and Australia to tackle global issues such as trafficking, terrorism and money laundering. Patricia believed in collaboration and often said, 'We don't succeed when we try to do it on our own, we have to reach out to others'. In 2010, she became the first female Secretary General of the Commonwealth, where she has served 53 countries and a combined population of 2.4 billion people! The impact of Patricia's advocacy and leadership speaks for itself and has been recognised with various awards, including the Dame of Merit. She is ranked one of the most influential Black Britons and was included on BBC's list of 100 Women in 2015.

REFLECTIVE SPACE

Not every piece of advice should be followed. How can you decide what's worth taking on or leaving behind?

What ways can you keep yourself motivated when others tell you to adjust or lower your expectations and ambitions?

WOMEN

beautifully & wonderfully made in the image of God!

Bishop, Chaplain to the Queen of England

Rose believed she was called to a life of ministry and serving humanity with her faith. But as a young girl, she did not see many women in leadership positions within the church. When she was 24 years old, the church began to ordain women as deacons, where previously women weren't allowed to practice.

Rose was recommended for the post, but some leaders felt she should focus on looking after her child and husband instead. They believed that Rose was incapable of doing both and that she had to choose between her calling and her family. Rose resisted, letting them know that her husband could very much look after himself and that she was fully capable of serving in ministry without neglecting her child.

Rose was ordained a deacon in a church in Wolverhampton. When she wanted to apply to become a priest, some leaders did not want to consider her for the position. They assumed a Black priest should only minister to Black people, but Rose knew she could provide leadership and support to anyone who might need it. She refused to let anyone put a limit on who her calling would reach. Women were not allowed to become priests until 1994, and Rose was one of the first women to step into this position. However, members of her church rejected her and some even resigned.

Because Rose was a woman, they did not consider her worthy to lead them or the church or to represent God. Still, Rose forged ahead, focusing on her work. She refused to be shaken, even when people rejected her from officiating at funerals because she was both Black and a woman. She placed her wellbeing and inner peace above anything else. Although she did not deny the pain of rejection, Rose would remind herself that she was worthy, chosen and capable to continue with her unique journey.

Twelve years later, she became the Bishop of Dover, where she used her position to challenge racial injustice within the Church. Rose was the first Black woman to become a bishop in the Church of England and the first Black priest to directly serve the Queen. She was also specially invited by the Duke and Duchess of Sussex, Meghan and Harry, to lead the prayers at their wedding, which was one of her greatest privileges. She campaigns for people of colour to be involved in the leadership of the church. More than anything, Rose wants Black women in leadership positions to be seen as normal. She remains one of the change agents making sure that the faith community in Britain is inclusive of women and truly reflects the people it serves. Rose calls herself a 'one-day-at-a-time girl'. Every day she chooses to focus on doing what she loves, in the best way that she can.

REFLECTIVE SPACE

What is your calling? Could you have more than one?

In your own words, write down a promise to remind yourself to have faith in your abilities and believe in your unique journey.

Malorie Blackman
1962

Children's Laureate
2013 - 2015

Noughts & Crosses
Hacker
Checkmate
Fangs
Chasing The Stars
Hostage
Thief
Robot Girl
Endgame
Double Cross
Pig Heart Boy

Author, Playwright

Malorie spent her childhood surrounded by words. She started writing her own stories and poems when she was seven, and as she grew up, she would spend every Saturday in the library reading all day. Malorie got her first job at 14 and was excited to finally buy her own books at her local bookshop — but she could never find a single book with children or young people who looked like her.

One day, she discovered a Black-owned bookshop in Islington where she picked up the *The Colour Purple*. It was written by a Black woman, Alice Walker, and told the story of a young Black girl called Celie. As Malorie read, her mind opened to new possibilities that changed her perspective forever. It was the first time she had read a book with a Black girl main character. She learned it was possible for Black women to be published while writing about the experiences, joys and sorrows of Black people. Malorie was inspired, so she picked up her pen and let her imagination run free across the page.

Malorie explored a variety of genres as she tried to find her writing niche. She attended writing workshops on horror stories and romance, and eventually found that writing for children was what she really wanted to do. She started writing picture books and sent them off to agents and publishers, but each one came back with a rejection. Once, Malorie thought she had a big break with a publisher.

They loved her story but asked her to change the identity of her main characters who were Black. The editors suggested her book would reach a wider audience if the characters were Asian instead. Besides, they said they were already publishing one book with a Black family. Malorie was insulted and disgusted that they thought they could only publish one book featuring Black characters, when there were already so many books with white characters. She refused to change her vision for her work. With each rejection letter, Malorie considered giving up on her writing dreams. But she decided to pay attention to the feedback she received. Over time, it became more encouraging. After more than two years of sending out her writing, 82 rejection letters and nine completed manuscripts, Malorie finally got a yes — someone wanted to publish her book!

Malorie has written more than 70 books, including the popular and award-winning Noughts & Crosses series, which was also adapted for TV. The story takes place in an alternate Britain where white people, the noughts, are the minority group and Black people, the crosses, are more privileged in society. Malorie set out to write the fantasy, mystery and thriller books she would have loved as a child — but with Black main characters. She believes that seeing yourself in stories validates your experiences, whether good or hard. Malorie's successful writing career has paved the way for many Black authors in Britain, and she has become one of Britain's most loved authors and a childhood hero for many.

REFLECTIVE SPACE

If you could write a book about any experience in your life, good or hard, what would it be?

Like Malorie, how can you present this story in a way that challenges assumptions and sparks interesting conversations?

The Melanated Royal

Philippa was born in the north of France to the Count and Countess of Hainault, William I and Joan. Her family was said to be of Black Moorish heritage, a diverse ethnic group of people that included Black African and Arab Muslims. The Black Moors were a powerful force across Europe, Africa, Asia and the Middle East. In England, King Edward II was in search of a bride for his son. He sent his trusted friend, Bishop Stapledon of Exeter, on a quest to meet Philippa and her family. When the Bishop returned to England, he gave the King a detailed description of Philippa's physical appearance, mentioning that her nose was somewhat broad and flat and her lips quite full. The young prince Edward was smitten. At the age of 17, Philippa was made Queen of England at Westminster Abbey. She took every opportunity to go on adventurous expeditions with her husband, King Edward III, through Europe and Scotland.

During the Hundred Years' War, Edward took siege of Calais in France for 11 months. He would allow nothing in or out of the city, and the people were starving. They ate anything to survive. Edward vowed to give the people food only after beheading six of their leaders.

Once Philippa heard of this, she became an advocate of peace and persuaded the king to spare them. She clothed the men, arranged a feast for them and sent them back home with presents for their family. Philippa may have been a young, courteous queen, but she possessed the strength of a quiet storm. In 1346, King Edward III left the country to go to war with the French and Philippa sat on the throne. Scottish King David II thought Edward's absence had weakened England's defences and he attacked. When Philippa realised the planned invasion, she mounted a white horse and summoned the British army to Neville's Cross. Philippa led the army to the battleground, building their courage with her powerful words. Although the British army was outnumbered by the Scottish, they fought in defence of their queen and won. Philippa continued to thrive and develop as a visionary leader. She was passionate about education, art and creative expression. The Queens College at the University of Oxford was founded in her honour. In turn, she ensured the college survived the financial challenges of its early days. In 1341, Philippa pushed for the college to have a small hospital with surrounding lands, so that it could be self-sufficient for the years to come. Her forward-thinking was one of the reasons that Queens College grew in prosperity throughout the 19th and 20th century.

REFLECTIVE SPACE

It can be challenging finding yourself in a foreign place and embracing a new nation as home, but Philippa still made an impact. List some of the attributes Philippa displayed.

How do you think they helped Philippa make her own way in England?

47

Nurse, Businesswoman

Mary spent her childhood in awe of her Jamaican mum, who was skilled in making traditional medicine and running several businesses. Mary mirrored her mother's every move. Whenever she observed her mum tending to hurt soldiers, she would run along and practise a similar procedure on her favourite doll. At 16, Mary's adventurous spirit inspired her to explore the world. With every trip she took, she improved on the medicinal skills her mum had taught her. Mary created herbal remedies that cured yellow fever and cholera, to aid the epidemics in Jamaica and California. Her reputation for her knowledge, healing touch and heart for the sick and wounded spread, but despite her success, she was often made to feel like she was not enough. In America, a white friend encouraged Mary to bleach her skin and make it even lighter so she would be accepted among any group of people. Mary responded, 'if I had been as dark, I would have been just as happy, as useful and as much respected by those whose respect I value'.

In October 1853, the Crimean War broke out. There was a shortage of food, medical supplies and medical staff. Mary was in London when she heard that Florence Nightingale needed additional nurses to help her tend to soldiers at the warfront. Mary went to the War Office to express her willingness to help, but in spite of her excellent track record of treating soldiers, the War Office turned her away.

Despite the rejection, she was determined to help and travelled around London borrowing money to stock up on medical supplies before boarding a ship to the Crimea. When she arrived, Mary used all her resources to set up a hospital closest to the warfront. She provided medicine and food not only to British soldiers but also the opposing side. To Mary, war was the enemy — not another human being.

When the British soldiers reclaimed Sevastopol, the army general approved Mary to carry medical supplies to the soldiers. As Mary walked through the gates, the first woman to do so since Britain's victory there, she was given a standing ovation and honoured for her service. *The Times* journalist William Russel travelled to the Crimea to interview her. When the war ended in 1856, Mary arrived back in London to find debt collectors knocking on her door, demanding back the money she had borrowed to set up a hospital in the Crimea. Mary was facing homelessness and poverty. William was horrified by what was happening and wrote a newspaper article challenging Britons to do better for the woman who has served its fallen. Once the article was published, support poured in from across the nation. The 'Mary Seacole Fund Grand Military Festival' was held in her honour at the Royal Surrey Gardens with 40,000 people present. Mary became a national hero and a marble bust of her was featured at the Royal Academy . Today, prizes, hospitals and even university buildings are named after her great legacy.

REFLECTIVE SPACE

- We can learn from anyone, anywhere. Name one person in your life who you can learn from by observing them doing their thing. Challenge yourself to reach out to them and spend some quality time learning from their knowledge.

- What does Mary's story say about how we can build knowledge beyond textbooks and being in class? In our day and age, how can you use the internet and social media to learn new skills and develop yourself? List three.

Writer, Journalist, Wartime BBC Broadcaster

Una's father passed away when she was ten. Due to financial difficulties, she was forced to leave school when her family moved to Kingston, which was more affordable. With her education cut short and no work experience, Una's job options were limited. She began volunteering in the field of social work, which exposed her to the inequality women faced in society. Una became curious about how power was created and maintained, and whether politics could bring about change. With her newfound curiosity came the desire for action. Una went from being a volunteer with no qualifications to the assistant editor of *The Jamaican Critic,* a journal that explored political issues. She dived into the world of journalism, taking every opportunity to develop her writing abilities. After three years of working on her craft, Una decided to launch her own magazine, *The Cosmopolitan,* dedicated to advocating for women's rights and improving women's access to education and the job market. Una adored words. As a journalist, she knew their power to invoke change in social opinion, and so she started to write poetry. Una wrote powerful poems like 'Black is Fancy' and 'Kinky Hair Blues' that challenged Eurocentric beauty standards and celebrated the beauty of Black skin and hair. It was her mission for Black women to feel beautiful in their own bodies. In addition to poems, she also wrote plays.

Her first play, *At What A Price,* had its opening night in London. It was a pioneering work of art and featured the first all–Black cast performance ever to be staged in the capital.

During World War I, the British government placed a colour bar on Black and Asian citizens of the British Empire, meaning people of colour could be refused entry into restaurants and pubs and even denied a home by landlords. Una partnered with the League of Coloured Peoples, a British civil rights organisation, to fight this discrimination. She also campaigned for Black nurses to be allowed to train in British hospitals. In many ways, her campaign work paved the way for incredible women like Kofoworola Abeni Pratt, who was the first black nurse to work in the National Health Service. In 1941, Una became the first Black female broadcaster on the BBC. She led a popular show called *Calling the West Indies* that helped many Black soldiers in the British Army connect with their loved ones in the West Indies. After a few years, Una created a new program called *Caribbean Voices* to raise awareness of how Black British people were helping on the war front and showcase their talents. This show introduced many Black artists, poets, and writers to the British public. Una was constantly brainstorming ways to push the Black British community forward. She shaped the world around her through her gifts of writing and speaking, whether it was writing a magazine, poem, play or petition.

REFLECTIVE SPACE

The written and spoken word is a powerful tool. Think of something you really care about and write a piece to express your thoughts.

How else can you use your writing and speaking abilities to make a change around you?

Lilian Bader
1918–2015

Royal Air Force Aircraft Technician

Lilian was born in Liverpool. Her father, who had served Britain in the Royal Navy during World War I, died in 1927, making her an orphan at only nine years old. Lilian was then separated from the only family members she had left, her two older brothers, when they left to fight for Britain in the war. Raised by nuns from then until she was 20 years old, Lilian entered the world anxious about the future and unsure of her prospects. She struggled to find employment once she left school. Her first job was with the Navy, Army and Air Forces Institutes during World War II. However, her job as a canteen lady was cut short because of her racial background. Due to the racist colour bar, discrimination based on race was allowed. When it was discovered that Lilian's father was of Bajan heritage, Lilian lost her job, even though her father had lost his life fighting for Britain.

To survive, Lilian took up random work, from hard labour on farms to working as a domestic servant. Then Lilian heard a radio announcement that Black people, who had been rejected from the army, were being interviewed to join the Royal Air Force.

Attitudes towards the colour bar were changing, though mainly it was because the government was desperate for help in the war effort. With a strong mind and heart determined to help her country, Lilian decided to apply. She became the first Black woman to join the British armed forces and took great pride in her job. As Lilian was getting used to her new life, she received devastating news that her older brother who had been serving in the Royal Navy had lost his life at sea. Lilian grieved her brother and sought ways to turn her pain into purpose. She took on a three-month challenge to train as an instrument repairer and upgrade her skills. Women were only just being allowed to train for this position and Lilian graduated top of her class. It was her responsibility to ensure there were no faults with the aircrafts that British soldiers would fly, and Lilian did her work with excellence. With her strong work ethic, Lilian scaled the ranks to become Acting Corporal! Lilian faced great difficulty trying to make her way through the world, from losing her father and her brothers to the war to facing rejection at work due to her race. But when a job presented itself, Lilian worked incredibly hard and rose up the ranks, making history as the first black British woman to join the Royal Air Force.

REFLECTIVE SPACE

Difficult challenges bring opportunities to learn and grow. Think about the last time you faced a difficult situation. How did the experience shape you?

When Lilian lost her brothers, a part of her grieving process was renewing her commitment to live intentionally and with purpose. What are some other ways you can cope with sadness or loss?

War Veteran, Medical Secretary

Constance Mark, fondly known as Connie, was born in Kingston, Jamaica. She was 19 when she joined the Royal Army Medical Corps as a senior medical secretary during World War II. Although young, Connie displayed undeniable leadership skills. Her primary duty was to write reports on all the battle injuries, and she was a whiz at bookkeeping. After six months, she was promoted to the military rank of Lance Corporal! A higher-ranking position brought more responsibility, and Connie embraced the challenge, confident that it would pay off in due time. Months later, she realised that she was not being paid her due in the new position. She began campaigning for a change in pay, but her requests were ignored. This was a key moment in Connie's journey — it was when she realised just how easily the hard work of Black women could go unrecognised and underpaid.

When World War II ended, Connie was recommended for the British Empire Medal for serving the Royal Medical Corps for almost a decade. However, this recommendation was ignored and Connie's contributions were belittled yet again. The British government made a call for its citizens to help rebuild the nation. Thousands of West Indians boarded a large ship called the *Empire Windrush* to heed the cry of the government.

Connie and her family were among those who moved to England, where she continued working as a medical secretary. Fearing that the service of Black Britons in the war effort would be overlooked, Connie created The Mary Seacole Memorial Association to honour Mary Seacole's legacy. But celebrating one amazing woman was not enough when so many other Black people had served the war effort. It was important to Connie that their legacy did not die with them.

As Britain prepared to celebrate the 50th anniversary of World War II in 1989, Connie started a campaign for this cause. She did not have enough money to fund it but found creative ways to raise money and also applied to the Greater London Arts Council for support. Her bookkeeping skills came in handy as she started research for the project, gathering as much evidence and photographs as possible. Connie went digging through the archives at the Imperial War Museum and arranged interviews with Black servicewomen and men until finally the exhibition was ready for the British public. Everyone was amazed at the memorial! In 1992, Connie finally received her British Empire Medal, and in 2001, the Queen awarded Connie with an Officer of the Order of British Empire (OBE). Connie would not stand by to let an entire group of people be erased from history and their efforts made invisible. She fought to keep the legacy of the brave alive. She was a Black woman who not only contributed to Britain but was determined that the legacy of others would not be forgotten.

REFLECTIVE SPACE

- Sometimes you have to ask for what you've earned, which can be scary. Practice how you might ask the next time this comes up.
- It is important to celebrate the sacrifices of those you love. What ways can you create a special memorial to remember their efforts?

55

Britain's First Black Policewoman

Sislin first trained as a nurse at Queen's Hospital in Croydon. One day while flipping through the local newspaper, she noticed an advert calling for more people to join the London Metropolitan Police. Life on the beat would be very different from the hectic hospital wards Sislin was familiar with, but she was optimistic about trying something new. In the early 1960s, very few Black people worked within the police force. In fact, the first ever Black male officer, Norwell Roberts, had joined the force only a year before. During that time, there were racial tensions between white people and Black West Indians following the Notting Hill Riots in 1958.

Many of Sislin's family and friends tried to discourage her from applying to the force. They feared she would not be accepted, worried for her safety and even felt betrayed that she was joining a service that they considered 'evil'. They refused to see that Sislin could champion for diversity and equality by going down the road less travelled and the change she could represent. Despite this lack of support, Sislin still applied, specifically writing on her application form that she was a Black woman.

After a gruelling interview and test, she arrived at the examination centre, disappointed to find she was the only Black woman there. On that day, she became the first Black woman to join the police force.

She reported for duty looking stunning and sharp in full uniform, and flashing press cameras captured every second of this historic moment. Some members of the British public were livid she had been appointed and expressed that they did not want a Black police officer. She received racist threats and hate mail, which was scary. But Sislin stayed strong, believing in the change she represented: The police force was finally becoming more diverse. Her first posting was in Croydon, a community she was familiar with and where she previously served as a nurse. After a year Sislin was promoted to a position in the famous police headquarters, Scotland Yard, and worked on the force until 1972. Sislin is an icon of progress and change. Words are powerful, especially when they come from those nearest and dearest to you. But Sislin's determination was stronger than the discouragement. She understood that racism and discrimination was, and still is, an issue within the police force, and she committed to changing it from within.

REFLECTIVE SPACE

◎ Words can form powerful motivators or distractors. How can you stay motivated when the people closest to you do not believe in your goal?

◎ What are some ways you can actively encourage others to follow their own dreams?

Black Women and Britain's Health Service

Sisterhood, Struggle and Hope

The lasting legacy of Black women on Britain's healthcare system is one that is not often told. In 1941, during World War II, Adenrele Ademola completed her training as a midwife at Guy's Hospital. Only three years later, Dr Irene Ighodaro completed her medical studies at Durham University and became Sierra Leone's first female doctor. The National Health Service (NHS) was established on 5 July 1948. World War II massively affected public services, and there was a huge shortage of hospital staff. Following the British government's invitation, thousands of Black nurses left their home countries to help rebuild British hospitals. Since then, Black nurses have migrated from across Africa and the Caribbean to work in the NHS, often providing healthcare to those living in deprived inner-city areas. There are countless examples of talented and impactful Black nurses — here are just a few.

Kofoworola Abeni Pratt

Kofoworola Abeni Pratt (1915–1992) was among the first Black nurses to staff the NHS. She came to Britain in 1946 and trained as a nurse despite the many barriers that Black women faced in the field. In 1950, she qualified as a state–registered nurse. Later, Kofoworola returned to her home country, Nigeria, to build a strong nursing practice there. She set up the first school of nursing in Ibadan. She also became the Chief Nursing Officer for Nigeria and the first Black woman to ever become Vice President of the International Council of Nurses. In 1973, Kofoworola was awarded the Florence Nightingale Medal, the highest international merit for a nurse, for her service to the profession.

Elizabeth Anionwu

Elizabeth Anionwu (1947) was born in Britain. She was inspired to become a nurse at the young age of four because of the tender care she received from nuns for her severe eczema. She trained as a community nurse tutor in Brent, caring for Black and other ethnic minority groups across London for many years.

During this time, she became aware of how severely sickle cell anaemia affected the African and Caribbean community. Determined to do something about it, Elizabeth set up a sickle cell centre in Brent in 1979. Here, Black people could receive information, counselling and access to screening services. She became Britain's first sickle cell and thalassaemia nurse specialist and helped set up Sickle Cell Society. Elizabeth became an Emeritus Professor of Nursing and has touched thousands of lives with her work. She was honoured by the Queen in 2017 with a Damehood.

Cecilia Akrisie Anim

Cecilia Akrisie Anim was born in Ghana and first trained as a midwife. She moved to Britain in the 1970s, where she retrained as a clinical nurse. Cecilia became the first Black person to be elected as the president of the Royal College of Nursing, the largest union of nurses in the world. She has received numerous honorary doctorates. In 2015, she was awarded the United Nations African Women of Excellence Award for her 30 year commitment to the NHS. The Queen also recognised Cecilia's service to healthcare and awarded her a Commander of the Most Excellent Order of the British Empire in 2016.

REFLECTIVE SPACE

Are there brave Black women in your life who have served in the NHS? My mum, Mrs Tejumade Oladapo, has worked in the NHS for over 20 years! How long have your sheroes supported the NHS? Ask them to share their experiences. If they could improve one thing, what would it be?

Come up with some ways you can appreciate them for their brave and consistent service.

They Changed the Nation

Almost 500,000 soldiers and civilians died in World War II. Britain was in crisis and had to look outward for help. The government called on people from across the Commonwealth to come to Britain's aid. They were needed to fill job shortages in transport services, hospitals, construction, manufacturing and other key industries. Many of the Black women in this book, like Connie Mark, had served Britain in the war and were happy to help rebuild the mother country. While other women, still little girls at the time, had their childhood shaped by the Windrush as their parents migrated to Britain to help in the rebuilding efforts and search for new opportunities. It is a pivotal part of Black British history and important to include in this book.

On 22 June 1948, the Empire Windrush ship arrived on British docks, having sailed from Jamaica. It carried over 490 Caribbean passengers who had been invited by the British government to live and work in Britain. This was the first of several trips that would happen between 1948 and 1970. Children travelled to Britain on their parents' passports as they did not yet have their own documents, making it tricky to pinpoint exactly how many people travelled during that time. But it is estimated that almost half a million people migrated to Britain to serve as essential workers.

The babies and young children who travelled aboard the Empire Windrush with their parents have since lived and worked in Britain, supporting the economy for decades. They are called the Windrush Generation, and many consider themselves faithful, hardworking British citizens.

In 2007, the British Home Office decided to enforce stricter policies on immigration. It did not matter if migrants were trying to escape war and persecution or searching for better opportunities for their children — the government refused to allow them into the country. Additionally, the government decided that anyone who was not British had to be deported. By 2012, they demanded that the NHS, banks, landlords and other services cooperate to push out migrants who did not have their documents. Suddenly, the Windrush generation were having their British identity questioned. Many of the organisations they helped save and build were now refusing to help them. The British government that had once invited them to live and work in the country was now questioning whether they had a right to call Britain their home.

Many of the Windrush generation were above the age of 60. They had come to Britain on their parents' passports and many of their parents had passed away. Now they were faced with an impossible task of proving they were British citizens. Some searched for pictures from their childhood or school days to prove they had lived here all along, but even that was not enough. Others struggled to find any evidence and were required to report to an immigration centre every fortnight. Some were evicted from their homes, denied access to their own hard-earned money by banks and were refused medical treatment by the NHS. They were arrested in their homes, separated from their families and held in detention centres. The repercussions were devastating for the Windrush generation: they lost their homes, jobs, families and had their identities stripped away as some were deported. For many of these brave Black British people, justice has still not been served.

REFLECTIVE SPACE

- Before now, had you heard about the Windrush Generation?
- What surprises you the most about their experience?
- What do you think justice for the Windrush Generation should look like?
- Write a letter to the Home Secretary and outline your thoughts on the best approach.

30 Black and Brave

Phillis Wheatley
Poet

Fanny Eaton
Victorian Model

Evelyn Dove
Cabaret Queen

Pauline Henriques
Actress

Tessa Sanderson
Olympic Gold Athlete

Anne Wafula Strike
Paralympic Wheelchair Racer

Dido Elizabeth Belle
Protégée to the Lord Chief Justice

Mary Prince
Abolitionist

Linda Dobbs
UK's First Black High Court Judge

Valerie Amos
First Black UK University Director

Patricia Scotland
QC Barrister and Secretary-General

Rose Hudson-Wilkin
First Black Female Bishop, Chaplain to Queen

Lilian Bader
Royal Air Force Aircraft Technician

Connie Mark
War Veteran

Sislin Fay Allen
Britain's First Black Policewoman

British Sheroes

Margaret Busby
Britain's Youngest Publisher

Amanda Aldridge
Opera Singer, Composer

Cassandra Walmer
Global Entertainer

Kanya King
Businesswoman, Founder

Claudia Jones
Activist

Gloria Cumper
Lawmaker

Olive Morris
Community Activist

Doreen Lawrence
Justice Campaigner

Malorie Blackman
Author

Queen Philippa
The Melanated Royal

Mary Seacole
Wartime BBC Broadcaster

Una Marson
Writer

Kofoworola Abeni Pratt
First Black Nurse to staff the NHS

Elizabeth Anionwu
Britain's First Sickle Cell Nurse Specialist

Cecilia Akrisie Anim
First Black President of Royal College of Nursing

Visit
www.anuadebogun.com
to download your
Free A2 Poster

Discover More!

The learning does not have to stop. Now, it's your turn.

A lot of reading, listening, watching and writing has gone into the production of this book. I found learning about these 30 sheroes and key moments in Black British history absolutely fascinating. I hope this book has inspired your curiosity to know more. Listed below are books, websites, interviews, projects and places you can explore to develop your knowledge. Have fun learning!

Reading

Adler, Sue (2008). *Baroness Scotland of Asthal: A Profile*. Tamarind Books, London.

Blackman, Malorie (2001). *Noughts and Crosses*. Penguin, London.

Bourne, Stephen (2016). *Evelyn Dove: Britain's Black Cabaret Queen*. Jacaranda Books, London.

— (2005). *Black in the British Frame: The Black Experience in British Film and Television*, 2nd edn. Continuum, London.

Bryan, Beverley, Stella Dadzie and Suzanne Scafe, (2018). *The Heart of the Race: Black Women's Lives in Britain*. Verso Books, London.

Busby, Margaret, ed. (2019). *New Daughters of Africa: An International Anthology of Writing by Women of African Descent*. Myriad Editions, Brighton.

Byrne, Paula (2014). Belle: *The True Story of Dido Belle*. William Collins, London.

Cumper, Patricia (1999). *One Bright Child*. BlackAmber Books, London.

Fryer, Peter (2018). *Staying Power: The History of Black People in Britain*, 3rd edn. Pluto Press, London.

Fuller, Sophie (1994). *The Pandora Guide to Women Composers: Britain and the United States 1629–Present*. Rivers Oram Press, London.

Jarret–Macauley, Delia (1998). *The Life of Una Marson, 1905–1965*. Manchester University Press, Manchester.

Lawrence, Doreen (2011). *And Still I Rise*. Faber & Faber, London.

Ogilvy, Julia (2014). *Women in Waiting: Prejudice at the Heart of the Church*. Bloomsbury Publishing, London.

Pines, Jim (1992). *Black and White in Colour, Black People in British Television since 1936*. BFI Publishing, London.

Prince, Mary, ed. by Moira Ferguson (1997). *The History of Mary Prince: A West Indian Slave*, revised edn. University of Michigan Press, Ann Arbor, MI.

Robinson, Jane (2019). *Mary Seacole: The Charismatic Black Nurse Who Became a Heroine of the Crimea*. Hachette, London.

Sanderson, Tessa (1986). Tessa: My Life in Athletics. Willow Books, Birmingham.

Seacole, Mary (2005). The Wonderful Adventures of Mrs Seacole in Many Lands. Penguin Classics, London.

Vernon, Patrick and Angelina Osborn (2020). *100 Great Black Britons*. Little, Brown, London.

Wafula–Strike, Anne (2010). *In My Dreams I Dance*. HarperTrue, London.

Wheatley, Phillis (2001). *Complete Writings*. Penguin Classics, London.

Websites

100 Great Black Britons:
100greatblackbritons.com

Africans in Yorkshire Project:
africansinyorkshireproject.com

BLAM UK CIC: blamuk.org
Second World War Digital Living Memorial:
Livingmemorial.org.uk

RARA Education Project:
raraeducationproject.org

Watch

Belle (2013).
Black Nurses: The Women Who Saved The NHS (2016).
First 100 Years: Baroness Scotland Biography (2019).
First 100 Years: Dame Linda Dobbs Biography (2019).

Places and Projects

The Africa Centre
Black Cultural Archives
Black History Walks
The British Library
The Grounded Project (BLAM UK CIC)
International Slavery Museum
Museum of London
Museumavnd – National Caribbean Heritage Museum
National Jazz Archive
The National Archives
Young Historians Project

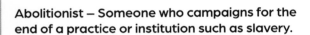

Glosssary

Abolitionist — Someone who campaigns for the end of a practice or institution such as slavery.

Apartheid — An Afrikaans word meaning 'separateness'; describes a system of discrimination based on race that occurred in South Africa.

Barrister — A lawyer that specialises in courtroom advocacy.

British Empire — A group of countries that were ruled or controlled by the British Crown.

CBE — Commander of the Most Excellent Order of the British Empire; an award given by the Queen of England to recognise the bravery and service of individuals in Britain.

Charwoman — A woman employed as a cleaner.
Civilian — An everyday person who is not a member of the military.

Colony — A land, territory or country controlled by another country.

Colour bar — A system where non-white people were denied access to the same opportunities and facilities that white people enjoyed.

Commonwealth — An association of countries that were once part of the British Empire.

Damehood — An honorific title given by the Queen and the female equivalent of a Knighthood.

Deportation — Forcing a foreigner to leave a country that they do not have the legal right to be in.

Detention centre — An institution designed to keep non-citizens in custody.
Discrimination — The unjust treatment of people based on the grounds of their race, gender, disability, age or other categories.

Eurocentric — A focus on European culture that excludes a wider view of the world.

Immigration centre — A location where non-citizens of a country, such as refugees, asylum seekers and migrants, are held in custody.

Inequality — The state of not being equal in status, rights and opportunities.

Institutional racism — Racism that is embedded as normal practice in society or within an organisation.

Jim Crow laws — Local and state laws that enforced racial segregation in the Southern states in America during the mid-20th century.

Justice of the Peace — A magistrate appointed by the Crown to provide justice in minor cases and keep peace within a specific district.

Legislation – A law that has been passed by Parliament.

Magistrate – A volunteer who hears minor court cases in their community.

Mammies – An American stereotype of Black women serving as a nanny or nurse to white children.

MBE – Member of the Most Excellent Order of the British Empire; an award given by the Queen of England to recognise the bravery and service of individuals in Britain.

Microaggression – Any incident, action or statement that subtly discriminates against a person from a marginalised group, whether because of their gender, race, class or any other aspect of their identity.

Migrant – A person who moves from place to place or attempts to relocate to a new country.

Migrate – To travel to one country, region or place from another.

Money laundering – Illegally obtaining large amounts of money through criminal activity and then trying to hide the criminal source of the money.

Mother country – Describes a country in relation to its colonies.

OBE – Officer of the Most Excellent Order of the British Empire; an award given by the Queen of England to recognise the bravery and service of individuals in Britain.

Persecution – Hostility against any individual based on their race, religious or political beliefs.

Political activist – A person who campaigns for social change and is actively involved in protest or political cause.

Private prosecution – A prosecution brought by a private individual not acting on behalf of the police.

Pro bono – A Latin phrase meaning 'for the public good' that describes professional work done without payment.

Pupillage – An apprenticeship that qualifies a person to be a member of the Bar and practise independently.

Regent – A person who governs the kingdom in the absence of the sovereign.

Regent – A person who governs the kingdom in the absence of the sovereign.

Segregation – The separation of a class, race or ethnic group through discriminatory means.

Sexism – Any discrimination based on the sex of the person.

Terrorism – The use of violence and force against civilians to intimidate the government or for a political cause.

Trafficking – Unlawfully transporting people to benefit from their service or work.

Selected Bibliography

Adams, Gene (1984). Dido Elizabeth Belle: A Black Girl at Kenwood: an account of a protegee of Lord Mansfield. *Camden History Review* 12.

Black History Studies. <blackhistorystudies.com>

Blakemore, Erin (2019). Who were the Moors? National Geographic History. <www.nationalgeographic.com/history/article/who-were-moors>

Brawley, Benjamin (1918). *The Negro in Literature and Art in the United States*. Duffield & Company, New York, NY.

Bourne, Stephen (2014). *Black Poppies: Britain's Black Community and the Great War*. The History Press, Cheltenham.

— (2014). Aldridge, Amanda Christina Elizabeth [pseud. Montague Ring]. *Oxford Dictionary of National Biography.*

— (1998). Obituary: Pauline Henriques. *The Independent*. <www.independent.co.uk/arts-entertainment/obituary-pauline-henri-ques-1186251.html>

Charles, Asselin (2016). Belle, Dido Elizabeth. *Oxford African American Studies Center.*

Cousins, Emily (2010). The Notting Hill Riots (1958). Black Past. <www.blackpast.org/global-african-history/notting-hill-riots-1958/>

Curry, Peter (2018). What was the role of Britain's Women in World War One? History Hit. <www.historyhit.com/what-was-the-role-of-women-in-world-war-one/>

(2015). Development Issues No. 1: Concepts of Inequality. United Nations. <www.un.org/en/development/desa/policy/wess/wess_dev_issues/dsp_policy_01.pdf>

The Fallen. UK Parliament. <www.parliament.uk/business/publications/research/olympic-britain/crime-and-defence/the-fallen/>

Gill, Dawn, Barbara Mayor and Maud Blair, ed. (1991). *Racism and Education: Structures and Strategies*. SAGE Publications, London.

Haikara, Nina (2020). Black History Month: Gloria Carpenter was a pioneer who helped bring legal change to the Caribbean. University of Toronto News. <www.utoronto.ca/news/black-history-month-gloria-carpenter-was-pioneer-who-helped-bring-legal-change-caribbean>

Jefferies, Stuart (2014). Dido Belle: the artworld enigma who inspired a movie. *The Guardian*. <www.theguardian.com/artanddesign/2014/may/27/dido-belle-enigmatic-painting-that-inspired-a-movie>

Katsha, Habiba (2020). Meet Kanya King, the woman behind the MOBO Awards. gal-dem. <gal-dem.com/kanya-king-interview-mobo-awards-founder-2020/>

Law, Kate (2020). Black Women in Britain During the Great War By Stephen Bourne. Women's History Network. <womenshistorynetwork.org/black-women-in-britain-during-the-great-war-by-stephen-bourne/>

The Life of Mary Seacole. BBC Teach. <www.bbc.co.uk/teach/school-radio/history-ks2-mary-seacole-video/zbphxyc>

Marshall, Herbert and Mildred Stock (1968). *Ira Aldridge: The Negro Tragedian*. Southern Illinois University Press, Carbondale, IL.

Murden, Sarah (2018). Dido Elizabeth Belle – A new perspective on her portrait. All Things Georgian. <georgianera.wordpress.com/2018/05/15/art-detectives-a-new-perspective-on-the-portrait-of-dido-elizabeth-belle/>

NHS at 70: Valuing the rich history of black and minority ethnic staff. NHS at 70. <www.nhs70.org.uk/story/nhs-70-valuing-rich-history-black-and-minority-ethnic-staff>

Remembering the Women of the Windrush Generation. Roman Candle Productions. <romancandleproductions.com/remembering-the-women-of-the-widrush-generation/>

(2016). The Story of Una Marson – Jamaican Writer, Feminist and International Activist. everlivingroots. <everlivingroots.wordpress.com/2016/11/18/the-story-of-una-marson-jamaican-writer-feminist-and-international-activist/>

Technician: Leading Aircraftwoman Lilian Bader. Royal Air Force Museum. <www.raf-museum.org.uk/research/online-exhibitions/pilots-of-the-caribbean/heroes-and-sheroes/technician-leading-aircraftwoman-lilian-bader.aspx>

Tomlinson, Lisa (2016). Una Marson: Cultural and Literary Nationalist. Black Perspectives. <www.aaihs.org/una-marson/>

West Indies Calling (1944).

Whale, Sebastian (2018). Doreen Lawrence: the mother who changed the nation. PoliticsHome. <www.politicshome.com/thehouse/article/doreen-lawrence-the-mother-who-changed-the-nation>

Wheatley, Phillis, and Margaretta Matilda Odell (1834). *Memoir and Poems of Phillis Wheatly: A Native African and a Slave*. Geo W. Light.

Women in the World War I. The National WWI Museum and Memorial. <www.theworldwar.org/learn/women>

Acknowledgments

This book would have been impossible to write without the brave Black sheroes whose incredible journeys are held in its pages. I honour them and the many other Black British women whose humanity, brilliance and diligence has shaken up Britain and the world. Thank you all for shinning so bright.

This book could have very well stayed an idea or just a manuscript tidily tucked away in my laptop if not for the loud and affirming support of the beautiful souls I am blessed to know: My exceptional beta readers, Suad and Stephanie, for their time, enthusiasm and helpful suggestions. Josephine Oluyitan, for the wonderful and vibrant illustrations that fill up this book. Monica Paterson, for the books' colourful interior design and layout. Mr Chindah, for his wise and witty counsel and for relentlessly pursuing the books' completion. Chimzi, Chris, Cedric and Janet for bringing a much-needed unique perspective to the book design process.

My not-so-little brothers, Timothy and Emmanuel, for their excitement towards this project and always believing in their big sis. My parents, Mr Oladimeji and Mrs Tejumade Oladapo, for their many sacrifices, which ground me, and lift me; you inspire me to bring my best — always. My love and best friend, Dr A.J Adebogun: Thank you for coming on this journey with me, and for all you've invested into this book. All your brainstorming, researching and encouragement; you amaze me.

To Abba, my guiding light, thank you for your patience with me.

Anu Adebogun

About the Author

Anu Adebogun is a British-Nigerian author, educator, researcher and award-winning youth advocate. Anu is purposeful about amplifying the voices of girls and women, championing student wellbeing and taking action against all forms of gender-based violence. Recognised by the Universal Peace Federation UK for her work, Anu has campaigned and partnered with leading UK national organisations to deliver sessions to thousands of young people to promote their safety, wellbeing and access to education. She is a trustee and advisory board member of several charities and community projects serving young people of minority or marginalised background. She holds a first-class law degree and completed an MSc in Criminology and Criminal Justice from the University of Oxford as a Kalisher Trust Scholar. Anu continues with doctoral study at Oxford University while writing to educate, elevate and inspire.

@ Anu Adebogun
www.anuadebogun.com

Printed in Great Britain
by Amazon